Dark Card

Dark Card

Becky Foust

Texas Review Press
Huntsville, TX

FIRST EDITION, 2008
Requests for permission to reproduce material from this work should be sent
to:

Permissions
Texas Review Press
English Department
Sam Houston State University
Huntsville, TX 77341-2146

Acknowledgments:

Grateful acknowledgment is made to the following journals that first printing
these poems, sometimes in altered form:

Ars Medica: "The Peripheral Becomes Crucial"
Atlanta Review: "Asperger Ecstasy"
Clackamas Literary Review: "Begin Again," "Empathy," "Homage to Teachers,"
    "Hope," "Refrigerator Mom," "Show Your Work," "Unstrung
    Instrument"
Journal of the American Medical Association: "Head Injury Odyssey"
Margie/The American Journal of Poetry: "Apologies To My OB-GYN,"
    "Dark Card"
Mudfish: "No Longer Medusa"
Red Rock Review: "Perfect Target," "Underneath"
South Carolina Review: "Like Dostoyevsky's," "Lucky"
Wordgathering: A Journal of Disability Poetry: "Eighteen," "The Visitation"

Cover Art by Lorna Stevens at www.lornastevens.com and Richard Lang
at www.sfelectricworks.com. Author photo by Donna Goldman at www.
buzzpictures.com

Library of Congress Cataloging-in-Publication Data

Foust, Rebecca, 1957-
   Dark card / Rebecca Foust. -- 1st ed.
   p. cm.
   ISBN-13: 978-1-933896-14-4 (pbk. : alk. paper)
   ISBN-10: 1-933896-14-0 (pbk. : alk. paper)
   1. Exceptional children--Poetry. 2. Children with disabilities--Poetry. 3. Parenting--
Poetry. I. Title.
   PS3606.O846D37 2007
   811'.6--dc22

                              2007042149

This book is dedicated to Mathew Lippman, teacher, believer, and friend, and to Linda Watanabe McFerrin, the first person to use the word "poet" in any proximity to my name. I am indebted to Molly Peacock for her guidance and encouragement in the final stages of manuscript revision, to Barry Spacks and Molly Fisk for their early reads, and to Susan Griffin and Peter Campion for their teaching and support. My family and friends have my unending love and gratitude for their tolerance of my work schedule. Finally, I must thank my son, whose courage and grace under fire have beeen my daily inspiration.

CONTENTS

Dark Card

DARK CARD

When they look at my son like that
at the grocery store check out
or at school assemblies,
I wait for the right moment, till they move
through laughter, raised eyebrows, clamped lips
—but before fear. Then I switch gears,
go into my tap dance-and-shuffle routine.

Yes, he's different, all kids are different, him
just a little bit more—oh, he's knocked down
the applesauce pyramid? So sorry, here,
my sleeves conceal napkins for messes like this,
and I can make them disappear. But before I do,
make sure you marvel at how the jars
made an algorithm when he pulled that one free.

Oh, he was standing on his desk again, crowing
like a rooster in your third-period class?
Yes, bad manners, and worse luck
that he noticed how today's date and the clock
matched the hour of what you taught
last week in a footnote—the exact pivotal
second of the Chinese Year of the Cock.

Before they get angry, I pull out my deck,
deal out what they want. Yes, he's different,
but look at his IQ score, his Math SAT!
I've figured out that difference pays freight
when linked with intelligence; genius trumps odd,
alchemizes bizarre into merely eccentric.
So I play the dark card of the idiot savant,

trotting out parlor tricks in physics and math:

he sees solutions the way you might breathe!
Or perceive! The color green! It's my ploy
to exorcise their pitchforks and torches,
to conjure Bill Gates when they see him,
or Einstein, not Kaczynski or Columbine;
perhaps they'll think him delightfully odd

or oddly delightful, dark Anime eyes,
brow arc calligraphy on rice paper skin,
his question mark flowerstalk spine.
But it's a swindle, a flimflam, a lie,
a not-celebration of what he sees
with his inward-turned eye:
the patterns in everything—traffic, dirt piles,

bare branches of trees, matrices in jar stacks,
Shang Dynasty history in tick of school clock,
music in color and math, the way shoppers
shuffle their feet while waiting on line;
how he tastes minute differences between brands—
even batches-within-brands—of pickles and cheese;
how he sees the moonlit vole
on the freeway's blurred berm.

TOO SOON

It's not my fault my doctor says
that my cervix is incompetent
a thousand ways, or that the DES
prescribed for mom's miscarriages
merely deferred them to me.

Now here I lie on my left side,
mandolin belly for the moment alive
with my restless son; my hands make a cradle
rocking him, rocking him early to sleep.

My labor heaves up in great waves
like the moon-crazed tide;
it raves like the tide-crazed moon,
rising and rising too soon, too soon.

My doctor looks young and afraid;
The nurse asks me if I've ever prayed.
I can't get my breath—
my gown's soaked with milk,
all spilt.

PALACE EUNUCH

You work in the palace of God
charged with the guard
of his most precious treasure,
the inventory of innocents,
but you've grown drunk
with power, forget who you are.
You spoke with the authority
to give or take life,
but your voice squeaked
when you asked
wouldn't I rather go home,
just go on home,
just have my baby at home.

Don't say you were trying to be kind,
you ball-less prick soft dick eunuch
cowardly coin-counting conservator.
You were practically pissing yourself
in your fear of malpractice,
you were shaking
in your green paper booties.

THAT SPACE

between
relief
you were out
and what
was supposed
to be—joy
that skip-beat
of nothing

between
nurse frozen
hand-over-mouth
and your
stopped-up cry,
blanknoise
motion
vacuum

silent sea
whitegreenwhite
scrub blur,
everything
for one
instant
in-between
everything,

hope up
en pointe on
its compass foot,
balancing
life against
death,

everything
arabesque,

unity of
held breath.

FIRSTBORN

wedged in that narrow,
seconds-ticking, desperate place,
cord Gordian-knotted

around your throat,
the doctor's ohfuckingshit
when he lifted it, and

it broke; your blood
on his face, my face, the ceiling
the back wall.

You, through the thicket
of green scrubs, splayed out
on the white butcher-papered table,

pale hair nimbusing your blue
Gandhi face; the expansion
and dominion of silence.

The reed
frail
wail
when
you
breathed.

APOLOGIES TO MY OB-GYN

Sorry that my boy birthed himself
too early, took up so much room
in your prenatal nursery
with his two pounds, two ounces
and did not oblige your nurses
with easy veins.

Sorry we were such pains in your ass
asking you to answer our night calls like that,
and that he did everything so backwards:
lost weight, gained fluid
blew up like a human balloon
then shriveled.

Sorry about how he defied your prognoses,
skyrocketed premiums, weighted the costs
in your cost-benefit analyses,
skewed bell-curve predictions
into one long, straight line;
sorry he took so much of your time

being so determined to live. He spent
today saving hopeless-case nymph moths
trapped in the porchlight, one matrix-dot
at a time, and now he's asleep; blue wingbeat
pulse fluttering his left temple—there,
there again. Just like it did then.

NO LONGER MEDUSA

When I had you I gave birth
to my mirror,
the chink in my armor.

Once I turned men to adamantine
with a glance, dove from cliffs
into dark quarries, swung grapevines
over ravines, rode arcs of tall birch trees
into the ground. Now I am alive

all night with fear for you, undone
by your sweet, milky breath,
the bobcat tufts on your ears,
your pink ribbon gums.
You freeze my heart to stone
when I measure your foot with my thumb.

UNREACHABLE CHILD

Don't go away from me like that,
eyes all dark and diffused,
to that dreamland of dew-soft fields
encircled by mist-mantled mountains
small superhero you with ham-size fists
stuck on those twig-size arms,
flying to a place where you're strong,
not afraid of the open door to your closet,
or phantoms that fragment and drift
when you part the hanging clothes.

I can help with the monster in the closet;
please let me help
with the monster in the closet.

What do you see behind your wide-open
dream-blind eyes, what dumb-bully night-terror
yanks you awake, sweats you
and chatters your teeth? What demon grins
and writhes shut every grammar school door?
Who are the lovely ones that charm you to wood,
leave you dreaming alone on the rug
every recess? It's hard to protect you
when you're not here, it's hard
to know what to do, whether to try to make true

what may not be awry—is it disability
or just the difference in intensity
that makes turquoise not quite blue?

INSTRUMENT

That
bewildered
look in
your eyes,

the hours
spent liberating
School Project
Butterflies,

your
baffled, raging,
muted-coronet
pain; how you

hated rain
but loved
sun, loved
to shout out,

run and climb on
anything—
until they
taught you to sit

on the rug,
dumbed
your shout-singing
tongue,

instructed
you in the art
of staying
unstrung.

PERFECT TARGET

—how they'd leer when he walked up
to them with his face flower-open, then
one would shrug a book-ballasted backpack
to sprawl him out flat on the asphalt.

How they'd tell him that the teacher
wanted, no really wanted him to jump
on the lunch table to see if it would break,
the apology note after note after note

he dutifully wrote. How at bath time
he'd say the bruises and scrapes were
Nothing, nothing, leave it alone,
Mom, don't make it worse, Mom.

How one time they cornered him
behind the storage shed and stoned him
in a hail of green oranges, left him
facedown bloodsnotted in dirt.

How he braided in three strands the lanyard
of his middle school years;
the hours and hours spent pacing
the playground alone,

the play dates and parties
he was never invited to, the chairs
pulled away
just before he sat down.

SWEET HEART

Swollen with beating and hot
with breath-rich blood,
what was taken first,

ripped from ribcage basket-rack,
riven, darkly drenched
and hung on Friday's cross

his exotic, limpid heart
a salty sweetcake crammed
in dingo's mouth—that ravening pack

of playground boys—a mere gateau
consumed in lust of fear and heat,
thrum and sing of blood in ear.

THE VISITATION

He eats the Almanac
whole, then
re-reads it
page-by-page
in his mind.

He finds the
arrowhead,
the dropped contact lens,
the long-lost
diamond ring.

He makes
meaning from acorns,
the sky,
knotted bits
of string.

He's gifted,
but he never asked for
that special
mark of blood
on his door,

that forehead-
touch-chin flash
of fire; he never
invited
the giver in.

HE NEVER LIES

not because he won't
or doesn't know better,
or how, he just can't.
I imagine him telling
too much of a truth,
or hellbent on one
of his endless
circular dissents,
the spiraling descent
into his own brand
of ineluctable logic—

Mom, you say that
you aren't the only one
who thinks
I should shave
but you are the one
saying it, so it's only
your opinion
even if you say
that you aren't
the only one who
thinks I should shave—

I fear he'll be over blunt
or otherwise by accident
draw their attention,
their anger, their rage;
I fear how far they
might go to assuage
their discomfort
with difference;
I imagine him drugged

or locked down on a ward;
in my nightmares
he's caged.

EIGHTEEN

Maybe I don't have to whisk
the ice smooth ahead of your
curling stone, explain
how you don't always mean

what you say, nor say what
you mean; tell why you don't cry
even though you feel pain,
explain your indifference

to rain. Or sun. How when
you get wet, sometimes
you burn. You're learning
to manage on your own,

how to keep track of taking
your meds, where and when
to get more, how much
and whether you took them

today. You're beginning
to take time from screen time
to eat, brush your teeth
and shave your luxurious beard,

you remember to set your
alarm. Charge your phone
in case your friends call.
Your friends. Your friends call.

BEGIN AGAIN

You think
the worst
is over,

that there's
nothing
left

to learn,
disbelieve,
believe,
endure.

You think
yourself
inured
to darkpath
worstcase fear.

But when they
find his bike
parked
at the bridge—

he was the
same age
as your son—

you begin
again
to dream

that dream

you thought
was done

of boys
who climb
the spans

and fall
like leaves
or swans.

REFRIGERATOR MOM

They called them cold and withholding
"refrigerator mothers," indicted them
with their kids' autism. You did it too,
you soul-less suck of a self-righteous
so-called psychologist, with your "walks

outside" and "your talks up in trees"
that never leafed out. You wasted time
sitting mute next to my son's muteness
for two years getting other work done,
explained how my "helicopter-mothering"

was causing the problems, how maybe
I was the one that ought to be medicated.
It was convenient for a time having me
Paxiled; no more second-guessing
the doctor's advice to chill out, no more

nagging about homework, chores,
computer, TV. I learned the art of aloof,
how to sleep while awake, how to
speak softly or not speak at all, how not
to feel desire or desire to weep.

For nearly a year in our house,
a kind of peace reigned, until one day
it cracked and rained pieces
of everything—propellers, coils, struts,
random refrigerator parts.

SOMETIMES THE MOLE IS MERELY

Sometimes they happen—bombs
blow up school buses, a son's shyness
is autism, the mole is more than a mole,
a teenager mistakes the brake for the gas

and that sound like a recycle truck drop-gate
where no truck should be and you run, you run
outside and see in the back wall of the garage
the cartoon-cutout shape the size of a car,
but the color of sky.

And when you stop and look through,
the car lolls on its back like a beetle, dazed
and still. Except that wheels still spin slowly
and inside, upside down, slowly swing

two freighted baskets of husband and son
suspended in seatbelts
that unbuckle to release them
in heaps; but this time, thank God,

heaps that move, unfold, extend,
crawl out flattened window frames,
stand up and walk out,
shivering off shards.

LUCKY

When we shake hands hello,
Aaron, yours lies damp
and limp in my palm,
like a broke-neck bird.

No light on your brow,
large little one—just that
five o'clock shadowed
biscuit-dough chin

and pink, wet lip under
stillpond eyes
with no texture of weather,
so flat and calm they perturb.

Your mom told me how
your brain starved for oxygen,
the cord that cinched your neck
a second too long

for you to be normal, and
not long enough to finish
you off. You weren't lucky
like my son, his nuchal cord lifted

in time, at least closer to in time,
than yours was, the doctor's
between-my-legs fumbling
to get just one finger under that noose,

my son's face blue, then suffused
pink, his damburst release
of pent breath.

HEAD INJURY ODYSSEY

Prepare as if for an ocean voyage, the doctor said
after their son's accident, gather your loaves of bread
and flagons of wine; make peace with your Gods.

But he didn't say they'd be sailing a balsa-wood
boat, or that their boy would be foundering too,
somewhere ahead in the mist

at the helm of his own fragile skiff; that they'd
separate in storms and boiling straits
not once, twice, but endless times

choosing between equally untenable tacks,
or that he'd be bound to the mast, ears sealed
with wax to slip past the Sirens singing

promises of no more pain, that he'd be
enchanted to stone by Calypso, forget home,
would have to sail the last leg alone;

that memory would be swallowed whole,
lost in whirlpools, caves, forests of pine,
so many animals slaughtered, so much wine

poured out on dry ground; or that when
he came home he'd be changed, so that they'd
have to keep looking for signs to know him by

—no one knew if his birthmark was there
under the great, new scar or would Bill his old dog
rise from his bed to meet him at the door.

SHOW YOUR WORK

My son is not good at emotion,
or doing things just to ease
understanding; there has to be
a reason that makes sense to him;
he does not usually notice
when people are displeased.

In preschool, his peers
absorbed social hierarchies
and nonverbal cues, but
he showed a preference
for algorithms.

In math class he got D's
for not showing his work.
He must have cheated, right?
Because no one can understand
a theorem without proving it,
especially not the teachers

who harassed him until we
caved and forced him
to learn the discipline
of showing his work;
hours and hours of sitting

at the dining room table
hunched over each sweaty,
scrawled page with the slow,
wayward pencil gripped
at the odd angle,
to lay down the evidence

for an answer he'd grasped
in an intake of breath.
We said he'd be glad later
when the math got too hard
to do in his head. He smiled

when I asked him years later
and told me the work he'd labored
to lay out was not even his own
but was made-up, his theory

of what he imagined the rest of us
needed to do to see the answer

that came to him whole, unbidden
like the moon on the horizon.
I don't do math, so in my mind
the work showed
goes something like this:

(-) small-talking
(-) planning
(-) reviewing your day
(-) worrying about the thousand details
that do not concern this problem
+ look inward
+ get up from your chair
+ walk through the dark house
+ climb each step to the back deck door
+ feel the latch
+ slide the bolt
+ walk into the clarity
and stillness
of the dark night air where
_____
= it is possible, finally to look up and stare
at pi in an infinity of moon.

UNDERNEATH

His face is blank as a kettle pond
dawn, but he feels everything
there is underneath—

tadpoles, minnows, sunfish, perch,
fish-hooks, tangled lines,
frays of fatyarn algae strands,

filaments tethering lily stars
that from above seem free to skim,
milky writhe of swimmers' legs,

mossed undersides of floats,
surprising truth of sailboat keels,
their iceberg depth.

ASPERGER ECSTASY

The excitement in the difference between two pennies
increases exponentially when there are twenty,
a hundred; a thousand, and he vibrates with joy.

It can be tying flies under a microscope, knot patterns
the size of this period. It can be cataloging washing
machine brands or the note variations in a symphony,
or committing to memory for joyous recounting
the entire year's schedule for the El-train.

Or picking up rocks from the road, distinguishing the
ones
that were indigenous from the gravel trucked in;
beach detritus—what wealth lays strewn—infinite variety
of shell, pebble, seaweed and broken bits of broken bits
of stones.

Oh, never to grow bored or experience a numbing
sameness of things! To immerse consciousness
in the sensory present of a bottle cap flattened by traffic,
or spend a whole school day with a paperclip stylus
carving whorls and curlicues in acorns, given
to the teacher instead of the worksheet—

each minute difference an opportunity point
on which another difference can hook
and turn and spread again; a thought diagram
of the branches that split and re-split,
blooming a pattern so rich

and complex it quickly becomes chaos to us—
and he's never happier than when.

LIKE DOSTOYEVSKY'S

idiot saint, wielding power
in oblivion; like Lee's Boo Radley
making gifts of treasured bits of trash;
like Williams' Laura Wingfield's
glass menagerie, how it
could be counted on for happiness.

My boy loves who he is,
even if the world does not
appreciate how he fills his days
with keyboard tapping, rereading his
inscrutable D & D books
and pacing and humming.

Everyone else is the problem.
Guileless as a kettle pond,
Prince Mishkin never planned
to ensnare the hurt feelings
and hearts that trailed after him.
Boo loved Indian head pennies

and pieces of string,
and made imaginary friends
with real children. Laura found
more than just comfort;
there was a kind of actual joy
in the repetitive thing.

My illiterate heart
is a mother's heart that beats
and breaks by rote, but I'm learning
to let him alone and to see
that his pacing and humming
are how he keeps time

in a world made of chaos,
the candle he lights in old night,
how he knits up the frayed cord-end
of every missed synapse,
into something coherent
that sings.

HOMAGE TO TEACHERS

Ring the bell for Ms. Ruto,
gentle and neutral when she described
him sitting on the first grade rug

facing this way while the rest
of the class faced that way;
Ring it for Doc, who piled desk

on desk in the room's center
and let the kids climb up to sail their
own Mayflower; who grinned

at our conferences, saying
you've got a live one! Ring
the bell for Ms. Stone, who

debunked the acronym disorders—
ADHD, ODD, OCD—saying school
is the problem; he needs to be

John Muir roaming the fields
with binoculars, and he's trapped
in my classroom.

And ring a last carillon
for Dr. Hart, who took him aside
in high school Chem to confide

that her brain worked exactly like
his brain worked, then made him her TA,
the job coveted by Honors Students

applying to Stanford, but for my son
the reason he went back to school,
learned how to set his alarm.

HOPE

I
Mom starting the
New York Times
crossword the day
she moved to hospice,
the Sunday puzzle

II
The measuring tape
my 12-year-old son
keeps in his bedroom

III
Pap buying corn
on the cob
at the roadside farm stand,
his teeth in his pocket

IV
That thing with feathers ED
was talking about, that will
against all odds
go aloft

V
Bill the dog at the door
where there's never
been a bone

VI
Dad going for the
dog track Trifecta
with his last
forty bucks

VII
Ms. Stone smiling
when we sat down
for our parent conference

VIII
heart carbonation;
maybe it's not
an infarction

IX
the exact shade of pink-red
of the bare-branched
flowering quince

X
my friend Gerard
getting a girlfriend

XI
spring after nuclear
winter; nucleus
of anything

XII
no third term
and they're not yet
all dead in Iraq

XIII
perhaps the pilot
won't err this time;
perhaps this time
the doctor is wrong.

EMPATHY

for Dr. Temple Grandin, autistic veterinarian

When she was little, visiting her
uncle and aunt's ranch, she liked
to get into the cattle press, flick
the lever to squeeze its sides in,

then she began to believe
she had a body, not just
a collection of electrons
repelling each other in space.

She was thought to lack empathy
for sad events, her classmates' tears,
but she noticed the other things
—rocks getting crushed, stars

that were dying. She hated how
cattle herded for slaughter would mill
about moaning, stamping their hooves,
would sometimes stampede

in eyerolling panic; she noticed
how they moved in the stockyards
to soothe themselves—in circles,
like water. She pondered her need

for pattern and order, how swinging
or rocking could calm her, and she
thought of a way to ease that ascension
to abattoir hell. She thought

of a ramp rising in widening circles,
like water. The feedlot execs could see

a PR trend, so they put the ramps in.
But they didn't see much more than

customers feeling sorry for cows;
not what Aquinas saw, that cruelty
to animals diminishes the human.
They did not, like Temple, wear

bovine skin, snort blood and fear,
flick flies with her tail, speak
with her doomed brethren
in Angus and Brahmin.

THE PERIPHERAL BECOMES CRUCIAL

in ways we'd never have guessed, like when
they unwound the crocodile-mummy shroud
focusing on what was within,

casting aside as trash the papyri cartonnage,
which when kicked, unscrolled to reveal
what Sappho wrote.

Sometimes more is inscribed
in the chemical signature of mud
than in the Sanskrit writ on the pot.

My son is gentler with moths
than people ever were with him,
and he chooses truth like breath.

He sets out cutlery backwards at table,
every time; he shaman-finds the bird point
flint, the fish spine, the speckled egg.

We watch as the linen-strip, tight-wrap coil
of that Gordian-knot neck-throttled curse,
that gene-encrypted, linked-chain curse,

that DES-taken-by-his-grandmother curse,
that fumble-fingered-fool-doctor-shaped curse,
unravels with his years, unwinds, unfolds,

lets loop out in vast uncoiling spirals
whole archives of text,
found worlds.